DEFINING AMERICA

QUESTIONS FOR EVERY AMERICAN

JIM SACK

Defining America is dedicated to Eileen, Adam, Josh, Chelsea, Emily, and Aaron who deserve to live in the best version of America.

ACKNOWLEDGMENTS

There are really too many people to acknowledge simply because so many individuals, groups, etc. have sparked ideas for what to include in this book. Whether it's politicians, celebrities, newspaper articles, family members, or former students, the ideas that are discussed here had to come from somewhere, I guess.

I do want to mention one person who probably doesn't even remember me, let alone the impact she's had in my working life. Many years ago, I was taking classes for my Masters Degree in Special Education and was working as a Teacher Assistant at a school for children with neurological disabilities. A supervisor there by the name of Suman S. Joshi once told me that I was very good at asking questions. She may have been hinting that I didn't have any answers, but I always took it as a compliment.

ALSO BY JIM SACK

The **What Makes Me...series** shares how a child's experiences and
relationships shape who they are- all told through their own words.

What Makes Me...Paula

What Makes Me...Rory

What Makes Me...Keisha

What Makes Me...Aaron

The Case of the Missing Trophy

*There's a free copy waiting for you at www.jimsack.com

The Real Classroom uses stories and lessons contributed by teachers, parents,
and former students to show what really goes on in school.

We're all busy with family, jobs, and life in general, but I'd really appreciate it
if you'd take just a minute or two to leave a review on Amazon! Even a single
sentence would be greatly appreciated!

Thanks!😄

Jim

CONTENTS

INTRODUCTION

Authors write for many reasons and choose their writing path based on those reasons. I always try to recognize and understand different connections and perspectives so my first book was intended to share what teaching was all about and my *What Makes Me...* series explores how kid's experiences shape their early years.

Defining America is different. It's the book that I felt I had to write in order to address issues facing all Americans every day. To be honest, I'm frustrated with what I see, read, and hear in this country and I felt that, in some ways, we need to start from scratch and figure out what America is all about.

1

USING THIS BOOK

You will find that there are many questions in this book and very few answers. The biggest challenge for me as the author was in trying to maintain a neutral position and not share my own viewpoints. I guarantee that I tried my best. I also guarantee that, in some ways, I failed.

I suppose I see this book as more of a "tool" to be used. Choose any topic that you may find interesting or start at the beginning if you prefer. There's no rhyme or reason to the order of the topics and some, or many, may not appeal to you. If you'd like, use this book to initiate a conversation with family members, friends, or classmates. You may find value in the opinions of others. On the other hand, if tempers flare, you may want to think about these questions by yourself.

Finally, I encourage you to keep an open mind- and for many of us, that can be a tall order!

2

THE WHITE HORSE

I wrote this essay a number of years ago when I was first starting to think about what America meant to me when I was younger. I think it still applies, although it appears that my image of our country was seen through rose colored glasses. This "rosy" image of the United States was enhanced by my being a teacher, I think. I sincerely believed that teachers were cheery people who loved working with kids and would always set a good example for students. I felt the same way when I became a parent. That meant being honest, not using foul language, and being a good role model for my kids. I had those same expectations for all adults. Now retired from teaching and after decades working with, and associating with, many people from all walks of life, I still try to have that same rosy outlook, but it's been tempered some- ok, maybe a lot. Anyway, this is what I thought back then.

When I was growing up, America was the good guy. We were the country that did the right thing. Other countries wanted to be like us, people around the world wanted to move here, and millions did just that. It seemed like only people in countries that didn't let their citizens leave wouldn't want to become Americans. This was for good reason. We were the good guys and like the good guys in the cowboy shows and movies I watched growing up, like Hopalong Cassidy and The Lone Ranger, the good guys rode a white horse.

Having been born in 1955, I grew up mostly in the 60's and 70's. I know there was turmoil during those decades because I watched the news with anchors such as David Brinkley, Walter Cronkite, Chet Huntley, Peter Jennings, and Dan Rather. To me, though, the turmoil and protests of those years were really about making America even better. The United States welcomed people from around the world to enjoy our freedoms. It didn't matter what you looked like or what religion you were- you were welcome here. Race relations seemed better- we even made fun of racist attitudes when we watched Archie Bunker in the 80's. The American dream, which to me began with growing up while balancing school and play before getting a job and beginning your own family, was alive and well. You and your wife bought a house and had two or three kids and you probably also had a dog. This was, after all, the land of opportunity.

Of course, I knew that America wasn't perfect. Race relations were still a problem and the "N" word was heard frequently, including in my neighborhood and community. Some families seemed to live in poorer neighborhoods and some kids dressed nicer than others. I heard about crimes on the news and read about them in the paper. I knew America still seemed too willing to get involved in wars around the world- we had sort of a "Marshall Dillon" (for those of you who don't recognize this name, he was on "Gunsmoke", a western back in the 60's) complex I always thought- and we seemed to want to be our planet's town marshal. Still, although we weren't perfect, we were pretty close.

QUESTIONS:

What does it mean to be the "good guys"? Is that really a thing?

Were we really the good guys back in the 50's, 60's, and 70's when I was growing up?

Are we now/still the good guys? As I write this, it's 2024. Racial issues, conflicts or wars in the Middle East and Ukraine, crime, immigration, gun violence, health care, inflation, and climate change are among today's many issues. Still...

Is the American Dream that I envisioned then still a possibility?

How would my attitudes be different towards America if I was Black? How about if I was female? What if my family had just immigrated to the United States?

What's your version of the American dream?

THE CONSTITUTION OF THE UNITED STATES OF AMERICA

We talk about the Constitution quite a bit, although I'm not convinced many of us know what's really in it or what it means. It's quite long so I'm not including the entire contents here, although I found this under the National Archives website and thought it was a proper summary of the Constitution.

"The Constitution acted like a colossal merger, uniting a group of states with different interests, laws, and cultures. Under America's first national government, the Articles of Confederation, the states acted together only for specific purposes. The Constitution united its citizens as members of a whole, vesting the power of the union in the people. Without it, the American Experiment might have ended as quickly as it had begun."

I also included the Preamble and the Bill of Rights since they are often referred to in discussions.

The Preamble To The United States Constitution

We the People of the United States, in Order to form a more perfect Union, establish Justice, insure domestic Tranquility, provide for the common defense, promote the general Welfare, and secure the Blessings of Liberty to ourselves and our Posterity, do ordain and establish this Constitution for the United States of America.

The Bill of Rights

First Amendment

Congress shall make no law respecting an establishment of religion, or prohibiting the free exercise thereof; or abridging the freedom of speech, or of the press; or the right of the people peaceably to assemble, and to petition the government for a redress of grievances.

Second Amendment

A well-regulated militia, being necessary to the security of a free state, the right of the people to keep and bear arms, shall not be infringed.

Third Amendment

No soldier shall, in time of peace be quartered in any house, without the consent of the owner, nor in time of war, but in a manner to be prescribed by law.

Fourth Amendment

The right of the people to be secure in their persons, houses, papers, and effects, against unreasonable searches and seizures, shall not be violated, and no warrants shall issue, but upon probable cause, supported by oath or affirmation, and particularly describing the place to be searched, and the persons or things to be seized.

Fifth Amendment

No person shall be held to answer for a capital, or otherwise infamous crime, unless on a presentment or indictment of a grand jury, except in cases arising in the land or naval forces, or in the militia, when in actual service in time of war or public danger; nor shall any person be subject for the same offense to be twice put in jeopardy of life or limb; nor shall be compelled in any criminal case to be a witness against himself, nor be deprived of life, liberty, or property, without due process of law; nor shall private property be taken for public use, without just compensation.

Sixth Amendment

In all criminal prosecutions, the accused shall enjoy the right to a speedy and public trial, by an impartial jury of the state and district wherein the crime shall have been committed, which district shall have been previously ascertained by law, and to be informed of the nature and cause of the accusation; to be confronted with the witnesses against him; to have compulsory process for obtaining witnesses in his favor, and to have the assistance of counsel for his defense.

Seventh Amendment

In suits at common law, where the value in controversy shall exceed twenty dollars, the right of trial by jury shall be preserved, and no fact tried by a jury, shall be otherwise reexamined in any court of the United States, than according to the rules of the common law.

Eighth Amendment

Excessive bail shall not be required, nor excessive fines imposed, nor cruel and unusual punishments inflicted.

Ninth Amendment

The enumeration in the Constitution, of certain rights, shall not be construed to deny or disparage others retained by the people.

Tenth Amendment

The powers not delegated to the United States by the Constitution, nor prohibited by it to the states, are reserved to the states respectively, or to the people.

QUESTIONS:

If you take a few minutes to read over the first ten amendments in the Bill of Rights, do you see how there can be different interpretations of those Amendments?

Which of these first ten amendments do you find to be most open to interpretation? Which do you find very clear in their stated purpose?

Certainly, this applies to the Second Amendment, but did you notice the phrase "nor cruel and unusual punishments inflicted" in the Eighth Amendment? Would that apply to the death penalty? Does that mean that the death penalty is unconstitutional?

This question may offend you, but is the Constitution outdated? After all, it was written over two hundred years ago. Is it time for a "rewrite"?

Do a little research regarding other Amendments to the Constitution after the first ten (the Bill of Rights). Are there any you disagree with or think should be changed in any way or even eliminated?? For example, the 22nd Amendment addresses term limits for Presidents. Should there be a limit on how many terms a person can serve as President?

4

PATRIOTISM

According to one dictionary, "patriotism" is defined as "the quality of being patriotic; devotion to and vigorous support for one's country"

I would guess that most of us feel as if we're patriotic. We might fly an American flag at our house, we may stand for the Star Spangled Banner when it's played at events, and we might celebrate Independence Day on July 4th.

QUESTIONS:

How do you, personally, define patriotism?

How does a person show how patriotic they are?

How about a politician? What are some examples of things a politician can do to demonstrate how patriotic they are? I remember when a politician was viewed as unpatriotic because they weren't wearing a certain pin on their jacket. If I'm a politician and I wear an American flag pin or some other similar symbol, does that mean I'm patriotic?

Should everyone be forced to stand when the Star Spangled Banner is playing? How about wearing a hat or placing their hand over their heart?

Is the reciting of the Pledge of Allegiance in schools still done? Should every child have to stand and say the Pledge, regardless of their families' beliefs or practices?

I remember when certain athletes raised their fists or refused to stand when the national anthem was being played or sung. Does that mean that they're not patriotic?

How about burning the flag of the United States? Should it be illegal? Can this act be considered an act of protest?

5

REQUIREMENTS TO BE THE PRESIDENT

According to the whitehouse.gov website, there are three requirements to be the President of the United States. They are that the individual is a natural born citizen of the United Sates, they must be at least thirty-five years of age, and that person must have lived in the United States for at least fourteen years. What are some other requirements that should be considered?

QUESTIONS:

We know that thirty-five years is the minimum age. Should there be a "maximum" age? I ask this, obviously, because of the ages of the two candidates that were expected to be the top contenders for the Presidency.

If you believe that there should be a maximum age to run for the Presidency, what should it be?

How about some kind of test to see if the candidate is mentally stable, or to test for intelligence?

Does "good character" enter into the discussion? How in the world would you be able to measure this when I don't think we can even agree on what "good character" is, let alone whether a candidate qualifies. However, in your opinion, what constitutes good character and should this be considered when choosing a president?

Although we may not want to publicly state whether a President should be of a particular race, gender, etc. how do you feel personally? Barack Obama was our first (and only) African American President and there has never been a female President, although Hillary Clinton was on the ballot in 2016 and Kamala Harris is running in the 2024 election.

Continuing with the tone of the previous question, how about a President who's Gay, Jewish, or Muslim? I seem to recall that John F. Kennedy was our first Catholic President, so voting for a candidate based on religion, sexual orientation, etc. may not be so farfetched.

6

SOCIAL MEDIA

Let me share the following: Just as I'm very limited in issues involving technology, I'm just as limited when it comes to knowledge concerning social media. I do have two facebook accounts, both a personal one and one as an author; an Instagram account that I rarely use; and an account with Linked In. However, I often have problems when posting, sharing the posts of others, etc. In other words, I'm one of those people who shouldn't have a cell phone, iPad, or computer of any kind, and shouldn't be on social media at all.

All that being said, I love the idea that I can keep in touch with people I probably wouldn't have contact with otherwise, I can get information from others having similar experiences, like traveling, and I'm friends with many people who I'd have lost contact with, like former students. However, there have been negative issues for users such as anxiety, bullying, and the amount of time individuals may spend on different platforms.

QUESTIONS:

How often do you use social media and for what length of time?

What social media platforms do you use on a regular basis?

Describe the purposes of each social media platform that you use. In other words, how do you use each of your preferred platforms?

Do you use social media for news of the day? What platform, if any, do you use for keeping up to date with current events? When you view something on social media, how do you know if it's true?

If you have children, do you use the same social media platforms?

If you have children, are you aware of their social media uses? Do you know what platforms they use and what content they're viewing?

Do you place any limits on their use of social media, whether by platform or specific content?

Regarding your own use of social media, do you use social media to "rant" about one issue or another? This could entail issues with a business, an employer, a neighbor, your child's teacher or school, etc.

If you do use social media to rant, do you first address the subject of your unhappiness directly, or do you head directly to social media to voice your displeasure?

As to what you share personally, are there topics or subjects that are "off limits"? In other words, are there limits to what you will share on social media? How about what you will view?

Have you ever felt jealous or envious of others because of what is posted on social media? As a personal example, I'm often jealous of friends who are traveling to locations I'd love to visit, but don't or can't.

Should the government have any involvement regarding social media platforms, their usage, etc.? I ask this question because of recent articles concerning TikTok.

How many social media platforms can you name? Can you list them in order from most popular with younger age children to most popular with senior citizens?

7

WHAT DO WE LOOK FOR WHEN IT COMES TO OUR POLITICAL LEADERS?

I believe that this is one of the most important chapters in this book for one specific reason. As Americans, we are at a crossroads and we must decide what we value in the people who will lead our country and be, arguably, the most powerful individuals in the world. This isn't like choosing our doctor or an electrician. This isn't like choosing what house we want to buy or where to go on vacation. Those decisions can be changed, mistakes can be made, and none are likely to be life-altering for others that are affected.

Choosing our political leaders, whether it be the President or those in other positions of power, require us to prioritize. Each American must decide what they value most in the individuals they vote for because those same individuals will be making decisions that affect our country for years and, possibly, decades.

The question that we all must answer is how do we find a balance between the positions or policies a politician supports and the character of that same politician. For that matter, should voters only look at policies and positions and not character, or is character more important?

Like in many other facets of human life, I used to see the world through rose colored glasses. I believed that a candidate's character, morals, and behavior came first. If I wasn't comfortable supporting that candidate as a person, how could I then vote for him or her in an election? I suppose I still feel that way, but it may be that I'm in the minority concerning this issue.

QUESTIONS:

In choosing our elected leaders, what are our main priorities? In other words, what do we look for in voting for a candidate?

If an elected leader gets things done, why would we care about their personality?

How do we know if the people we plan on voting for are telling the truth?

Where do we get our information from regarding news stories about candidates?

Do we want a President who we can relate to? How important is it that the candidate we vote for is like us?

Does it matter whether a candidate is smarter than you are? Is a candidate who appears smarter than me an advantage as to whether I vote for that candidate or not?

Do we want a President who's like us or do we want a President who's different? If different, how should they be different?

How important is it if a candidate understands how our system of government really works?

I seem to recall a time when practicing a certain religion, being a certain gender, etc. would automatically eliminate a candidate from the presidency. Is that still the case? Should gender, race, age, etc. be factors when deciding who to vote for?

What negative characteristics would you say are so important to you that you would never vote for that person?

If a candidate has been accused of a crime, prosecuted for a crime, or convicted of a crime, does that affect your willingness to vote for that person? Which of those matters? Being accused? Prosecuted? Convicted? Do the circumstances matter, such as the type of offense or who has made the accusation? How so?

8

TERMS AND LABELS

Many of us seem to base our attitudes and opinions on certain words or phrases. We seem to love labeling things. We see them in the grocery store, the library, and department stores. My bookmarks on my computer help me to characterize websites I look at. The problem with labels isn't that they're not necessary, it's that we use them to pass judgement. Here are some labels that are currently in use. Can you define each term? Would those who feel differently give a different definition for each? I suggest you sit down with someone who sees things from a different viewpoint and compare your understanding of each term or phrase.

conservative
liberal
LGBTQ
socialist
replacement theory
gun nut
transgender/trans
politically correct
CRT (Critical Race Theory)
cancel culture

libs
woke
communist
MAGA
illegals
gerrymandering
DEI (Diversity, Equity, and Inclusion)

9

GUNS IN AMERICA

First, full disclosure:

I have quite a few friends and family members who are avid gun owners and I, personally, love to go to a shooting range where I've fired hand guns and rifles. (Feel free to invite me anytime!) That being said, I don't hunt, nor do I even kill any insects or bugs in my home (except ants and mosquitoes). I'm also working on becoming a vegetarian, although that's proving to be a difficult process.

Now, on to the topic at hand.

I could be wrong, but it seems that there are many more shootings in the United States now than there were when I was growing up. I'm not just talking about mass shootings that seem to occur on a regular basis. I'm also referring to everyday shootings that I read about happening everywhere. Law enforcement officers are often "outgunned", suicides with guns number in the thousands annually, and gun deaths now are the number one cause of deaths regarding children. Overall, I've read that between 30,000 and 40,000 Americans die each year in gun related deaths.

QUESTIONS:

Do we really have a gun problem in America? Considering that our population is somewhere between 330 and 340 million people, maybe the answer isn't that simple.

It's easy to say that, of course we have a gun problem. However, is the problem that we have too many guns or is it that we don't have enough guns? How could more guns and gun owners prevent gun deaths from happening?

It appears that millions of Americans are willing to accept gun deaths as the price to pay for individual rights. How do we balance individual rights with gun deaths?

What does the Second Amendment say exactly? (Hint: It's in the Bill of Rights listed above) It's only one sentence, but I bet most readers can't recite this amendment without looking so here it is again: "A well regulated Militia, being necessary to the security of a free State, the right of the people to keep and bear Arms, shall not be infringed."

Interpreting the Second Amendment to suit your view, such as when some emphasize the term "regulated militia" to encourage limits on gun ownership while others see the Second Amendment as justifying any gun purchase with no limits is not helpful simply because there is no clear answer. It comes down to interpretation. So, therefore, how do **you** interpret the Second Amendment?

How do we balance the rights of gun owners with those of people who don't support gun ownership? For example, if I own a hand gun and want to carry it while shopping or going to the movies, should I be allowed to do so? On the other hand, if I go shopping or see a movie, shouldn't I be allowed to do so without being steps away from someone who's armed with a handgun? (By the way, what about carrying a knife? Just something to think about.)

Recently, a local church held a raffle with the winner being able to choose between an AR-15 and a flame thrower. What do you think about this? Is this a suitable prize for a raffle? Should there be limits on who can enter a drawing such as this? What limits would be appropriate? Does the fact that a church is the organization that's organizing the give-a-way affect your opinions at all?

What do you think about a waiting period between the time an individual fills out any required paperwork (should there be any paperwork?) and when the gun may be picked up? Would eliminating any "spur of the moment decisions" have any effect on gun violence? I've read that suicides are a large percentage of the gun deaths in America each year. Would a mandatory waiting period reduce this number? How long of a waiting period should there be? Three days? Ten days?

What should be done, if anything, to address the number of children killed in gun-related incidents? Should parents be held accountable and, if so, under what circumstances? How about requiring that any firearms be locked in a secure cabinet? Should it depend on whether an adult is home?

What restrictions, if any, should there be on gun ownership, whether by age, type of weapon, training, etc.?

Over the years, I've seen numerous polls suggesting that the majority of Americans want universal background checks so law enforcement officials can trace a gun's owner in case it's used in a crime. What would background checks entail? What about giving a gun away or selling a gun privately? What, if any, background checks would there be in those circumstances?

10

DEMOCRATS VS. REPUBLICANS

I'd like to think that most people realize that you can't draw conclusions about someone just because of the political party they often support. I know that in my case I haven't always voted for candidates in a specific political party, although I usually vote for candidates in the same party.

That being said, I've had enough conversations with people to realize that Americans, as well as people in other countries around the world, tend to lump others into certain categories based on their political leanings.

For example, historically, many people's image of Democrats tends to suggest that they are noted for being the defenders of the poor and middle class. Democrats are also often viewed as being soft on crime. Republicans, on the other hand, are known for supporting limited government, but are also considered to be the party of the rich. Are any of these statements true at all or are they overblown exaggerations? My opinion is that you can't simply apply generalizations such as these to a specific party any more than you can to those who support that party. However, that's just my own view.

What do you see as the truth when it comes to our country's two main political parties? Now, before you answer, what proof do you have that your view is accurate? Have you done your own research? If so, how many sources have you used in your research and are all of them similar in philosophy?

For each of the following, which party do you consider the stronger one?

- addressing violent crime
- supportive of poor and middle class Americans
- supportive of upper class or wealthy Americans
- the belief that big government is needed to protect the interests of "regular citizens"
- reducing the size and scope of government
- fair tax rates
- supportive of unions
- supportive of non-union workers
- environmental issues
- addressing illegal immigration
- reducing the national debt
- maintaining good relationships with our allies
- lowering prices for everyday items, such as groceries
- supportive of abortion rights
- supportive of women's rights
- addressing inflation
- minority rights
- education
- mass shootings
- healthcare
- racism

I'm sure that I've missed quite a few topics that could also be included in this list. What are some of those and where do you think each political party stands?

QUESTIONS:

Do we really need political parties? Like many Americans, I would guess there is a feeling that politicians in both parties are more interested in pursuing party gains and limiting party losses than in representing Americans and making America a better place to live. How would our political systems change if parties were eliminated?

Should we add one or more parties? If so, what would be the priorities of a new party/parties? Where is the need? What would be the goals?

What would need to happen for one or more "new" political parties to become serious contenders for voters to consider? In other words, how do we ensure that candidates from these so called "fringe" parties actually have a chance to be elected.

What would our political landscape look like if there were no political parties?

11

PUNCHING BAGS

Let me begin with a story. When I was around ten, there was a family living nearby who had foster kids. One of those kids was a girl with very frizzy hair who went to our elementary school, but was in the "special class", which was where the kids who had special needs went. One day on the bus, some kids were picking on her so I got up and sat next to her to stop the bullying. Now, I don't share that to brag and I'm certainly far from being brave (we won't talk about my fear of dark places). I will say, though, that I've always felt strongly about bullying. Also, I usually root for the underdog. I think it's possible that those two go together.

This chapter is about those who, like that girl on the bus, I refer to as "punching bags". They are the individuals, groups, or occupations that seem to draw widespread criticism. It seems, at times, that it is the popular action to target them possibly because they're easy targets or it makes us feel good about our own situation. In some cases, it may help us to explain our own financial difficulties or personal struggles. It may even be something as simple as a reason why our favorite team lost a game.

Here is my list of "punching bags".

·   ·   ·

The Internal Revenue Service (the IRS): To be honest, I've never had any involvement with the IRS. I've never been audited and I just pay my taxes each year and wait to hear if I'll get a refund (now that I said that, you know I'll be audited next year). I just know that I constantly hear about those who view the IRS as the enemy and I often see commercials sponsored by different businesses promising to help you fight back against the IRS for trying to collect back taxes.

QUESTIONS:

Have you ever been audited? What were the results of the audit?

Why do you think so many people seem to dislike the IRS?

Why do so many politicians criticize the IRS? Why do they propose cuts to that particular agency?

Sports Officials: From children's leagues to the pros, sports officials seem to bring out the worst in people. A friend of ours who was a very mild mannered person became an obnoxious screaming parent when his child was playing soccer, loudly criticizing the officials, until he was kicked out of the stands during one game. I also remember a baseball official ejecting a coach after the coach's loud and constant complaining about calls made during a game. A person I know was a baseball umpire in a men's softball league and was constantly harassed in every game. As for the pros...

QUESTIONS:

When did our reactions turn from disagreeing with calls in games to threats and physical violence?

Whatever happened to setting a good example for our children?

Do you think these kinds of behaviors are related to other forms of violence, threats, bullying, etc.?

. . .

The Federal Bureau of Investigation (the FBI): Let me begin with a story. When I was graduating high school, a friend asked if he could use me as a reference for future jobs and, of course, I said yes. To be honest, I was probably seventeen and didn't give it much thought. A few years later, I got a phone call from a nearby FBI office asking me (telling me?) that they wanted to meet with me. Now, I was immediately concerned and couldn't imagine why the FBI wanted to see me. It turned out that my friend had applied for a position and I was listed as a reference. By the way, in case you were wondering, he got the job!

QUESTIONS:

Like the IRS, I've never had a bad experience with the FBI. Have you had any contact with them? If so, was it a positive experience or a negative one?

Other than what you hear from politicians, what evidence do you have that the FBI acts in a lawful way or not?

The Police (I'm referring to all law enforcement except for Federal agencies): I'm sure you're not surprised, but I have another story. Growing up, I watched a lot of police shows on TV and when I was in college, I thought of a career in law enforcement. I contacted police departments in half a dozen cities around the country explaining my interest. Many years later, when I was probably in my forties or so, my wife and I were visiting my Mom and I brought this up. She told me that I had gotten a letter years ago from a police department. I expressed surprise and said I didn't remember any such letter. Mom replied that she ripped it up because she didn't want me to be a police officer and there was no need to continue the conversation. Honestly, I would've been lousy at that job anyway (dark places?).

QUESTIONS:

What contacts have you had with the police? Have you been arrested? Were you guilty of what you were arrested for?

Other than what you hear or read in social media, the news, etc. what are your opinions of the job police officers do? I'm referring to efficiency, courtesy, professionalism, etc.

Do you believe that police actions differ, depending on where you live, your ethnic background, your age, etc.?

The Media: Since the next chapter is on "The Media", I won't say too much here. I will say, however, that, in my opinion, "The Media" certainly qualifies as a popular punching bag in America.

Immigrants: I originally thought I would list "illegals" here, but really it's immigrants in general that are a punching bag for many. For a country that has always appeared to be a beacon for those wanting a better life, immigrants are now often used as a political tool and a target by many citizens.

QUESTIONS:

How can anyone tell the difference between someone who is here legally vs. someone who is here illegally?

Is it the right of any citizen to question the legal status of another person? How do you justify your feelings on this matter?

What does an immigrant look like? What does an "illegal" look like? That may sound like a silly question, but there have been numerous altercations, sometimes including violence, involving individuals who have been perceived as "illegal".

Do you believe that many crimes, both violent and non-violent, have been committed by people that are here illegally? What proof do you have to support such a view?

Is there a way to compare crime rates involving those who are here illegally vs. American citizens?

Do you feel differently about an immigrant from one part of the world than another? In other words, do you view an immigrant from a European country differently than an immigrant from a Middle Eastern country? How about an immigrant from a predominantly Spanish speaking country, an Asian country, etc.? What I'm trying to get at here, in case you haven't noticed, is whether a person's physical appearance or characteristics plays any part in how you view that person. Thoughts?

Homeless People: It would seem that those individuals who are homeless would generate sympathy, rather than scorn, resentment, or anger. However, homeless people have often been vied as scapegoats and been seen as a problem to be solved rather than individuals needing help.

QUESTIONS:

Do you know anyone who is, or has been, homeless? How have you reacted to their situation?

Why do you believe people are homeless?

What, if anything, have you done to address homelessness? Whose responsibility is it to address this situation?

Do you believe that some sort of housing should be offered to people who are homeless? Are you willing to have taxpayer dollars used for this purpose? How would you feel about a residence for homeless individuals and families located near where you live?

12

"THE" MEDIA

When I was growing up, there were only three primary television channels and each had their own anchors. Walter Cronkite, Peter Jennings, Dan Rather, and the team of Chet Huntley and David Brinkley were news anchors at different times and the channel you watched was pretty much determined by who you liked best since they often reported on the same events. Walter Cronkite, for example was often referred to as "the most trusted man in America". After all, facts were facts and there didn't appear to be any room for bias. As I write this, our exposure to the news can be very different because it isn't necessarily about the facts as much as "shaping" a story according to certain philosophies. Part of this, in my opinion, is because of the sheer number of news sources, ranging from mainstream news outlets to online reporting, as well as social media groups, etc.

It seems commonplace, or even popular nowadays, to blame "THE MEDIA" for just about every problem in America. THE MEDIA gives too much attention to some people or to certain issues. THE MEDIA is biased towards certain viewpoints so you can't believe the individuals or other sources reporting the news. In short, it's become popular for Americans to blame segments of THE MEDIA and to only view or listen to news sources that tell them what they want to hear.

QUESTIONS:

Who or what is THE MEDIA? How do you define THE MEDIA?

If those in THE MEDIA are responsible for reporting the news of the day, why are the accounts so different? You'd think that the news is based upon facts, wouldn't you?

Do most Americans follow media outlets that offer more of an unbiased viewpoint concerning current events or do we tend to follow outlets that seem to represent what we think is right? In other words, do you follow a media outlet because it's unbiased or do you follow the outlet that you tend to agree with?

Is there a difference between news shows and political commentary? For example, did you consider Rachel Maddow's show to be a news show or political commentary? How about Laura Ingraham?

Do facts matter? Who determines whether news reports contain facts? If a news outlet covers a story and reports news that is proven untrue are there consequences? Is that news outlet required to acknowledge their mistake? As the reader/viewer, are you interested in whether a report is true or are you just pleased that the news is reported in a way that you agree with?

Which of the following is your primary source of news?

- newspaper
- television networks
- mainstream online news outlets, such as the major networks
- social media
- online stories that come from outlets that aren't generally considered mainstream

If your choice of a news outlet shares a story that you don't agree with, do you no longer view or listen to that outlet?

Does the person reporting the news matter? In other words, how often do you still experience that news source if your preferred anchor, reporter, etc. is no longer with that news source?

13

RACE IN AMERICA

Let me begin with two stories. First, when I was an undergraduate in college, I sometimes went out with my friend, Julie. I should add that Julie is Black and I'm white. When we went out people often stared at us, we thought, because seeing a mixed race couple was not that common during the 70's (although, truthfully, it may have been because Julie was absolutely stunning and those "gawkers" may have been wondering why she was with me in the first place). Truth be told, we loved the attention. The second story took place when I was teaching third grade in a small rural school that was overwhelmingly white. I don't remember the issue that led to this conversation, but I asked my students to raise their hands if their parents would be upset if an older brother or sister began dating a Black boy or girl. Almost every student raised their hand. Would it have been the same if my students were mostly Black and I asked what they thought their parents reactions would be if their older brother or sister began dating a white boy or girl? I have no idea.

QUESTIONS:

How do you feel about interracial marriage? I suppose that most people would think in terms of a Black person marrying a white person, but what if it involved a person with Asian features, or one person who's Hispanic?

How do you feel about giving money as reparations to Black people? What about Native Americans or Japanese Americans?

This may seem like a weird question, but what grade would you give to our country when it comes to race relations. ie. A+ if America is in great shape regarding race issues, F if we are failing, or somewhere in between.

Do we still need affirmative action in order for minority students to get into college?

Why are most NFL players Black?

Why are most Major League Baseball players Hispanic?

Why do we not discuss American Indian problems? How about other minorities?

Why do we not discuss the treatment of Japanese Americans during World War II?

Can a Black person be a racist? Why do you believe that?

Is it ok to not be comfortable around people of a different color?

Is the proper term Native Americans or American Indians?

How do you feel about displaying figures of Confederate officers, slave owners, or the Confederate flag in public places? How about statues of famous historical figures who were later identified as slave owners? Should they remain on display?

We used to celebrate Columbus Day. Now, some states celebrate Indigenous People's Day. What do you think about that?

I read an article recently about the Fearless Fund, an organization that addresses the lack of access to venture capital for Black women by offering grants, mentorship, and resources. Is this a form of racial discrimination because the assistance provided by Fearless Fund is only provided to Black women? Then again, is it gender discrimination because it only is available to women?

Are white people victims of racism?

How would you define the word "racist"?

Is it ok to be a member of a group that has been labeled a White Supremacy group? Why or why not?

There are many groups that have been described as White Supremacy groups. One group says that they aren't a White Supremacy group, but believe that America is the rightful home to those whose ancestors were from Europe. Thoughts?

Is ANTIFA real? What, or who, is ANTIFA? How are they similar to White Supremacy groups? How are they different?

A number of years ago, I was talking with a white man we had hired as a painter and he used the "N" word. When I voiced my displeasure, he apologized and said he didn't mean anything by it and that it was used routinely where he was from. Thoughts?

Is racism only about color? Is antisemitism a form of racism? How about negative attitudes towards Asian-Americans or Native Americans?

14

BLAME IT ON MAYBERRY

I had this published in the Albany Times Union newspaper back in 2016. I'm especially proud of it because it was a featured "commentary", rather than a letter to the editor, which were more common. As much as I believed in it's message then, I think it's even more accurate eight years later and explains much of what's been happening in America. Then again, maybe not. Anyway, here's what I wrote:

"I think I've figured out why so many people in their 50's and older are angry about the current state of America. I also know who to blame. It's not really about today's politics or even Donald Trump that's led to this anger, nor is it about President Obama, the NRA, immigrants, terrorists, or the economy in general. If you dig deeper, as I have, you know that the blame for all of this anger begins in Mayberry.

I've always said that I wanted to live in Mayberry, that fictional town in North Carolina where Andy Taylor, Barney Fife, and their friends and family lived. It was peaceful and happy there. Nothing bad ever really happened, and if things headed in that direction, Sheriff Andy Taylor could figure things out. Life was simple and predictable.

Television shows like "The Andy Griffith Show", "Leave It to

Beaver", "The Donna Reed Show", and countless others painted a picture that, for millions of Americans, was one of the peaceful family life that was the American Dream. Dad went to work, Mom took care of the home, and the kids got into mischief of one kind or another, always working things out in the end. Unfortunately, these shows had some other things in common, and I believe they're part of a bigger picture that many Americans long for. In all of those shows, Dad had a job. In 2016, many Dads don't have a job or at least it doesn't pay enough, or even if Dad has a job and it pays well, Dad doesn't live with the family anyway. Mom might have a job, but it also might not pay enough and she might not be around, either. Where are the kids anyway? Who's watching them? Who's giving all of that parental advice that Opie received from his Pa? How about the homes these television families lived in? They lived in nice homes and I don't remember any of them having trouble making the mortgage payment. Hungry? Sick? It wasn't a problem for Andy, Opie, and Aunt Bee. This "simpler time" is what many of us long for. On tv at least, it was a time when families stuck together, there was respect and courtesy between neighbors and friends, and there was always a happy ending. I wanted to live in Mayberry. I guess I still do.

While these wholesome family shows illustrated what many of us saw as the American Dream, there was something missing for millions of American families. While white, middle class Americans enjoyed the peaceful existence in Mayberry, other families recognized the absence of African Americans, Hispanic Americans, and Asian Americans, in addition to other minorities. If religion was mentioned or referred to in any way, it was Christianity that took center stage, such as when Andy and Barney sang in the church choir. Men and women had certain roles and those roles didn't change. Immigrants? Not that I remember, legal or otherwise. In fact, like probably many others, I didn't realize back then how much was missing. It can be hard to see what isn't there.

I don't know how others felt about this simple view of America, but I looked with envy at those happy people who lived in Mayberry. I wanted to hang out at Floyd's Barbershop, get my toaster fixed at

Emmit's Fix It Shop, and sit on Andy's porch while listening to him play his guitar. I suppose it's impossible to know how much, if at all, Mayberry played a part in projecting an image of America that people miss. I just know that our country doesn't quite look the same as it did on tv when Andy and Barney patrolled the streets of Mayberry. At least we know who to blame now."

QUESTIONS:

Was life really simpler for you back in the 60's, 70's, and 80's? How was it simpler?

Do you think it was simpler for everyone? Did gender, race, etc. matter? How would you say that other people would answer that question?

15

IMMIGRATION

Images of the Statue of Liberty and Ellis Island, metaphors comparing America to a melting pot or a tossed salad encourage the notion that America is welcoming to all those who want to have a better life here. At least, that <u>was </u>the image many had for America. Now, I'm not so sure.

I think it's safe to say that immigration, as an issue, is at, or at least near, the top of the list when it comes to concerns for many Americans. It's also very far from a simple issue, not just because Americans disagree on solutions, but because we can't even agree on priorities regarding immigrants. We, as Americans, are concerned with new immigrants crossing the border to enter our country. However, there are also concerns with those immigrants who are already here in the United States, whether they are here illegally or not, as well as issues regarding children who have been here for years, sometimes with family members and sometimes not.

QUESTIONS:
What does the term "illegals" mean to you?
What is legal immigration?

What are three contributions made by those entering the country legally?

What are three negative consequences of immigration?

How do we go about identifying those individuals that are here in America illegally?

What do we do with those individuals who were born in this country, but whose parents have never been citizens?

How do you feel about some kind of national identification card for every American citizen? Could this be a way to identify those individuals, regardless of their appearance? How would you, personally, feel about carrying such a card?

What consequences should be in place, if any, for those who harbor or hire illegal immigrants?

Rank your concerns with immigration. Consider jobs, crime, housing, voting, and any other factors you can think of.

We always hear talk about our southern border. What about our northern border?

16

VOTING IN AMERICA

Being able to vote for candidates seems like a basic right of being an American citizen. It's at the very core of what our country is all about. So, how did we get to the point where there is such a discrepancy when it comes to attitudes we as Americans have regarding voting rights? In my case, being a white male means that I'm aware of the historical struggle that's existed regarding voting for people of color, but I haven't really experienced it. The same can be said for women, for example.

Voting, itself, begins for most of us as children, even though the stakes may not have been that high. Family members, including kids, may vote on such various subjects as what's for dinner or what television show to watch. As kids get a little older, there are elections for class officers in school and of course, voting in real "elections" even though those votes may not count. However, when a citizen is old enough to vote in a legally binding election, that's when it really matters.

QUESTIONS:

Is voting a privilege or a responsibility? Do you vote because it's your responsibility as an American citizen or do you vote because you have the right to vote?

Should voting be encouraged? If so, what can we do to encourage eligible citizens to vote? Is this where longer voting hours, more polling places, etc. come into play? Now, if you think that voting is a responsibility, maybe we aren't concerned with making it easier to vote. Potential voters will have to simply find a way to vote.

Let's look at HOW we vote. Currently, there are several methods when voting, including in person, vote by mail, online voting, etc. In addition, each state seems to have their own rules when it comes to voting methods used, voting hours, etc. Thoughts?

Should each state have their own voting rules and policies or should every state use the same voting methods, deadlines, and procedures for counting ballots when it comes to voting?

If voting by mail is allowed, should it be based on need, such as for those in the military, or should it be available to anyone who prefers to vote that way? What should be the rules concerning mail-in voting? If mail in ballots are accepted, should they be allowed to be counted after election day?

Should voters be required to present some kind of identification before being allowed to vote? What kind of id? Drivers license? Birth certificate? Please keep in mind that millions of Americans don't possess a driver's license and I'd guess that millions also wouldn't be able to produce their birth certificate.

How about early voting? Should voters be allowed to cast their ballots before election day? How much before? Does that also apply to mail in voting?

What do you think about online voting?

At what age should an individual be allowed to vote in local, state, and national elections? I remember a difference of opinion I once heard from two individuals who were discussing this and one felt that if you were old enough to enlist or be drafted, that means you should also be allowed to vote. Does this make sense? How about tying voting to the drinking age?

What are some rules you'd suggest when it comes to making sure that voters are eligible and votes are counted properly?

Should there be restrictions on when election results are reported since knowing early results from some states may influence voters in states where the polls are still open?

Would using time zones address the above issue so that polls in every state are open at the same time?

Let's switch gears a little. The Electoral College is the tool that we use when choosing our next president. Each state has a certain number of electoral votes, with some states referred to as "battleground states" because they're considered more crucial to a candidate winning.

I remember when I was teaching third grade that my students probably had a better understanding of the Electoral College than many adults in our country. Regardless, it seems that in every election one issue that arises is whether we should still be using this method to choose our next President.

QUESTIONS:

Do you feel that you have a clear understanding of the electoral college? If your answer is yes, than please explain the process to someone who doesn't, such as a child. If your answer is no, and assuming that you believe it's important to understand the electoral college, what can you do to learn more about this process?

Have you noticed that states that aren't considered "battleground states" are rarely spoken about during election season? For example, New York, my home state, is rarely discussed because it is known to be a "blue state" and almost always supports the Democratic candidate. Likewise, Texas is considered a "red state" and will most likely support the Republican candidate for President. Could things change in states that are considered solidly red or blue? Certainly it's possible, but how likely is it?

With the Electoral College deciding the outcome of the Presidential Election, why even have the popular vote? Other than being a talking point for candidates, what is gained by having and sharing the results of the popular vote?

What do you know about the voters in the Electoral College? Who are they? How does an individual become an elector? What part, if any, does party affiliation play in determining who become electors?

17

SEXUAL ORIENTATION IN AMERICA

I wouldn't have had a clue what the phrase "sexual orientation" meant when I was growing up. Boys went out with girls and eventually, for most, that led to marriage. That meant a man and woman getting married, having children, a house, and a dog (if they were lucky- I'm a dog lover) and remained married until one or both passed away.

To be honest, although I suppose it seemed simple at the time, I wonder how many kids and adults felt alone or misunderstood. Certainly, it was easier for those of us who I guess were in the majority, but I believe that many people didn't have it so "easy".

Like a number of chapters in this book, I fine myself ignorant in the questions I'm asking or in the phrasing I'm using. I expect that I'm not alone in feeling this way, but I also think it doesn't really make it any more acceptable.

QUESTIONS:
Do you know what these terms mean?

- LGBTQ (it took me a while to remember the order of the letters, let alone what each letter stands for)
- cisgender
- gay
- transgender
- heterosexual
- queer
- sexual orientation
- binary
- gender affirming care
- straight

Should Gay marriage be legal? Why or why not?

Should vendors, such as a baker or photographer, have a say as to who they choose to work with if the reasons have to do with a potential client being Gay? Does this also mean that the same vendor can choose not to work with someone because of their religious beliefs? How about if the vendor doesn't like that person's appearance? That last question may sound silly, but my point is when is it ok to "discriminate" against another person?

Think about the same questions in regards to an officiant for a wedding or a government official sought out for a marriage license. What then?

Have you been to a gay wedding? If not, how would you feel about attending?

Is it ok for a person to not like or accept people who are Gay?

How do you feel about Gay people adopting kids?

How do you determine what bathroom to use if the choice is either a Men's Room or Women's Room and you're Gay or Transgender?

Unless a person tells you that they are Gay or Transgender, how do you know?

Were there Gay people in the 1800's? How about the 1900's?

When you meet someone who refers to themselves as he/she, or them, how do you know how to address them?

18

ABORTION

Once again, let me begin with a story. As a teacher, I always prided myself as being able to present different sides of an issue, regardless of my personal feelings. I also always tried my best when answering questions from students, no matter what the question. I never ducked an issue. That is, except for the time when one of my third graders asked me what an abortion was. The problem with defining the term, abortion, is that you can't really define the word without being in the middle of the debate. I hate to admit it, but the only answer I could come up with was to recommend that they ask their parents for a definition. It wasn't my proudest moment as a teacher!

QUESTIONS:

How would you define what an abortion is? Do you think that your definition is the same as one given by your neighbors or friends?

Should there be a limit as to how many abortions one woman should be able to have?

Should decisions regarding abortion laws require women to be involved in those discussions? I say this because in cases I've read about, it seems as if men are the ones making decisions concerning abortion law.

Is there is a legal timeline as to when an abortion must be carried out? In other words, how late into a pregnancy can an abortion still be performed?

What if the father of the unborn child feels differently than the mother?

If abortions are outlawed in a particular state or nationwide, who is then responsible for raising that child? Are there supports in place?

If a state doesn't allow abortions, should there be limits on pregnant woman traveling elsewhere where abortions are available?

How about a pregnancy resulting from rape or incest?

Should men hold any responsibility for pregnancies? How would that work?

What do the terms "pro-life" and "pro-choice" mean?

What do you think about methods to end a pregnancy that do not involve an operation, such as a pill?

Should there be any penalties for those medical professionals who provide "support" for a pregnant mother? Does it depend on what the support is?

How about the age of an expectant mother? How does this affect that individual's rights?

19

NO ONE TALKS ANYMORE

On a somewhat lighter note, I wonder how much the lack of communication and understanding between people is due to how little we actually speak with one another these days. I blame (tongue in cheek) the following:

Self-serve gasoline- Not to date myself, but when I was a kid, my Mom pulled up to the pump and a nice man came out to pump our gas, check the oil, etc. We then paid him, waited for our change or credit card receipt, all while having minor exchanges with him about the weather, etc.

Online Banking and/or ATM Machines- How often do you actually go into a bank? Many of the services they provide are now done online, by using an ATM, or by drive-through.

Headphones- On a recent flight, a man took the seat next to me, put on a pair of headphones, and kept them on until we landed. Not that I wanted to be his best friend, but not a word was spoken.

Working From Home- Two of our kids work from home, at least part time, and we have friends who have stated how they can work from anywhere because they work online. That time may include videoconferencing, but it isn't the same as in-person contact.

Cell phones- Just about everyone has one (except someone I know named Carl), but are there times when they can be put away, ignored, or turned off? If you're with someone, especially your kids, why are you on your phone?

Restaurant orders online or by phone and pick up- We did this at Panera a couple of times. I understand the convenience, but I'd rather just walk in, order with a person, and then eat my food in the restaurant. I might even see someone I know. My wife and I recently went to McDonald's for breakfast (don't judge me). We ordered at the counter, got our food from a real person when our number was called, and sat there while we ate. Most people ordered from the kiosk, or at least tried.

Drive Through or Pick Up Food, Groceries, and Drugs- I know it's convenient, but it also leads to less face to face communication. You can order meals and groceries online, pull up to a restaurant or store, and someone will actually place your order in your vehicle, all without a word being spoken!

Food Delivery Services- When I was growing up, we'd occasionally have pizza delivered. Nowadays, people have meals and groceries delivered to their home.

Covid- Covid seemed to change everything. People wore masks (I, for one, not only didn't recognize friends or family members who were wearing one, but it also made communication tough, and that's if there was even an attempt at doing so) and avoided human contact when possible.

Self Serve Checkout- I go into some stores now and there are as many, or more, people using self checkout lines as there are people going through the regular lanes to pay for their purchases. I do this sometimes, too, and then I only talk to an employee when I don't know what I'm doing- which is more often than you'd think.

Shopping Online- If possible, I shop at a small business. If not, I may shop at a chain that is more regional, rather than national. If not, it's the national chain. Shopping online is my last choice, but I do it because of the convenience, wide range of choices, and the lower prices. I feel guilty then, but I still do it.

Internet Searches (we call it "ask the Google")- I hate to admit this, but I search the internet for everything from who's that person in that commercial and where have I seen them before to what is sleep apnea, how serious is it, and why do I need a CPAP machine. I won't even share how often I check out stories on my favorite sports teams and view tv bloopers. Besides, the 1962 World Book Encyclopedia I grew up with got mildewy and we had to get rid of it.

You Tube videos- Instead of stopping in your neighborhood business for advice, you can just view one of hundreds of videos on almost any given subject, including which electric toothbrush is best. Yeah, I know this to be true.

Online reservations for flights, hotels, restaurants, etc. I miss the days of calling an airline directly, talking to a real person, and asking for the cheapest flight available, the one where you have to sit on the wing. I know it's not funny, but I always said that to the airline rep I spoke with. Come to think of it, I don't remember any of them laughing.

Automatic car washes- We had one near us when we lived in Maine. You push a couple of buttons, pay with a card, and drive forward until the word STOP lights up. Then you sit there. I miss the guy taking my money after asking which wash I want and another guy pointing for me to move right or left so my tires go in the right way.

Automatic Headlights- This one sounds silly, but when I was younger, there were a few times when I noticed someone had left their headlights on in a parking lot. I'd check to see if their car was unlocked and if it was, I'd reach in and shut them off. I'd never do that now because many cars have headlights that turn off automatically. Also, between car alarms and many people expecting the worst, I don't want to get arrested.

20

DONALD TRUMP

Disclaimer: As I wrote in "Using This Book", **The biggest challenge for me as the author was in trying to maintain a neutral position and not share my own viewpoints. I guarantee that I tried my best.** This was the most challenging chapter for me to write.

In the early days of the 2016 election cycle after Donald Trump announced his candidacy, he took several actions that I was sure would end his campaign. Among them, he labeled all Mexicans as drug dealers, rapists, and murderers (other than a few good ones), he claimed that he couldn't release his taxes because of an audit, and he addressed other candidates with insulting nicknames and foul language. I honestly didn't think he'd go anywhere as a candidate for the Presidency. Obviously, I was wrong. In writing this book, I didn't initially plan on dedicating an entire chapter to one individual, but Trump is such a polarizing figure that I felt I had to. People tend to either love him or hate him. Some believe everything he says while others find it hard to believe that he's ever told the truth. Some refer to him as a conman and grifter, while others believe he is the victim of a corrupt system. Regardless of your personal feelings towards Donald Trump, he has played, and continues to play, a very strong role in the America that exists now and the country we're likely to have in the future.

To quote a famous President, "Let me make this perfectly clear". All of the problems and challenges I see in this country didn't begin with Donald Trump. Racism didn't begin with Trump. Gun violence didn't begin with him and neither did the growing income gap between the wealthiest Americans and everyone else. It's easy to blame Donald Trump for every problem that exists in this country, and many individuals do, but the challenges we face to truly make America the country that we want it to be are real and challenging, but did not originate with the election of Donald Trump.

It's important that Americans, as well as citizens in other countries, look not only at his comments and behaviors, but try to focus on the proposals and policies of this individual. That's why we each must look at his actions during his first term in office and his stated plans for a possible second term. There are many times when his detractors just cannot understand the appeal of Donald Trump. His supporters are often labeled ignorant, racist, or even violent. I remember the controversy when Hillary Clinton used the term "deplorable" in describing Trump supporters. However, the appeal of having someone other than a "career politician" lead our country is attractive to millions of Americans. The image that many have of our government is negative, the feeling being that little is accomplished because there's so much "gamesmanship" involved and politicians place party and personal gains over country. I believe that is primarily how Donald Trump was elected in the first place. He was viewed as a successful businessman and someone who was a "straight shooter", a man who would say what was on his mind. In other words, he sounded like "one of us".

Millions of Americans also supported the notion that an over abundance of regulations was to blame for the failure of American businesses. Trump and his administration removed vast numbers of these rules and regulations, with the goal being a stronger business climate. That image of "burdensome regulations", what many would refer to as "red tape", is quite appealing. In a related area, overhauling the tax code was really a winning formula because words like simple and the removal of the afore mentioned "red tape" was seen as a positive step.

Regardless of whether you love him or hate him, or somewhere in the middle, Donald Trump has certainly been a source of discussion and debate in America and around the world. I think practically all Americans believe that he was elected to the Presidency in 2016. That's probably the only thing Americans agree on concerning Donald Trump.

QUESTIONS:

Who won the Presidential election in 2016?

What evidence do you have that proves your belief?

Who won the Presidential election in 2020?

What evidence do you have that proves your belief?

The following is a test to see whether you're able to empathize with those who feel differently than you:

As polarizing a figure as he is, if you're **not** a fan of Donald Trump, are you able to name at least three personality traits or accomplishments in office that you admire?

If you **are** a supporter of Donald Trump, are you able to name at east three personality traits or accomplishments in office that you dislike or didn't agree with about him?

Finally, since Donald Trump has been convicted of a crime, should he still be eligible to run for president? Does this have any affect on whether you plan to vote for him?

21

LET'S BUILD A PRESIDENT

The President of the United States is almost universally considered the leader of the free world and one of the most powerful individuals on Earth. For the moment, let's forget who's currently running for the office and try to focus on a model of the perfect person for the position. Try very hard not to choose characteristics of previous Presidents or politicians you admired, or any specific person for that matter. Instead, think in terms of building a model. For this exercise, we're going to start with a clean slate- no restrictions, even those listed in the Constitution.

QUESTIONS:

What age range would you suggest?

- 20-29
- 30-39
- 40-49
- 50-59
- 60-69
- 70-79

- 80-89

Should the President be male or female?

How about the size of a President? Would a larger individual be viewed as more imposing, a stronger leader, etc.?

What religion, if any, should the President be? If you don't initially believe that this is a factor, how about a Jewish president? Muslim? Agnostic?

Does sexual orientation play a role in choosing the perfect President? Would you vote for someone who's Gay? Transgender?

Does your President have to be married? Would a divorce have any effect on your support? I remember a time when a person who'd been divorced had an uphill battle.

Should a President have children?

Does a President have to be born in the United States?

Do they have to be an American citizen?

How about a residency requirement? Assuming they live in America (?), is there a minimum number of years they must live here before becoming President?

How about a President's racial makeup? Black? White? Hispanic? Mixed race? Asian?

22

MONEY IN GOVERNMENT

In my opinion, there is no more pressing issue in the way our government works than in the flood of money involved in elections and the daily functioning of our government. The amount of money that is spent by candidates or on their behalf, often by sources outside the area a candidate is hoping to represent. is mind boggling. Also, my usual exhaustive research shows that members of Congress make $174,000 per year. How is it, then, that so many are millionaires? Were they millionaires before running for a Congressional seat? As to the daily workings in Congress, as well as state and local government, I believe that most Americans would say that money does indeed affect the decisions made by our government representatives.

QUESTIONS:

Are political campaigns the right length? Are they too short or too long? If there wasn't such an emphasis on fundraising, could/should political campaigns be shorter?

Should there be some kind of spending cap on elections so it's not a matter of which candidate can gather the most money to spend on a campaign?

Should the names of donors be made public? Should sharing donor's names publicly be based on how much that person donates?

It may be easy to want donor's to be made public, but do you want your neighbors, friends, employers, etc. to know whose campaign you're supporting financially?

How about spending caps? Should there be limits on how much an individual can donate to a campaign? How about a business?

Do you understand the Citizens United decision by the Supreme Court? Do you agree with it?

Do you know what a "PAC" is when it comes to political donations or fundraising? How about a Super PAC?

If a member of Congress receives money from those individuals or groups that support a certain position, should we assume that the money is to sway the individual's position or could it be that the donations are simply to thank that member for his/her actions?

A list of the top ten donors to the present presidential campaigns from a specific state shows amounts donated in the millions of dollars from each. Much of this money went to PACS and Super PACS that support specific candidates. One candidate held a fundraiser where some of the tickets to attend cost one million dollars per ticket. Does this not suggest a problem?

Would you support publicly financed elections where tax dollars only are used by candidates to fund their campaigns?

23

PRIORITIES

There are many issues facing Americans today, some of which have been concerns for many decades, such as foreign policy, while others are a little newer, such as climate change. As we make our decision as to which Presidential candidate to support, one factor to consider is which issue(s) do we care about the most? Then, I suppose we need to determine whether we agree with each candidates positions on these issues.

Where do you stand on which issues are most important to you, personally? One possible suggestion is to number them from "most important" to "least important". Another strategy is to give each issue a number from one to three, with the ones being the highest priority.

health care
immigration
America's role as world leader
climate change
education
abortion
gun control
budget deficit
campaign donations

racial equality
unemployment
maintaining a strong military
Gay marriage
affordable housing
maintaining good relations with our allies
cost of everyday goods, including groceries, gasoline, etc.

Which issues are at the top of your list?

24

VIOLENCE IN AMERICA

I struggled with where to place this topic because, to me, it may be related to gun violence, but, then again, it may not. When I was growing up, fights in school were rare, weapons used to commit violent acts were not as deadly as they seem to be now, and even crimes committed by adults seemed to involve less lethal weapons.

Is what I see as an increase in violence in America due to a specific factor or is it just a matter of Americans being more accepting of violent acts as just the way things are?

QUESTIONS:

Do television shows, movies, etc. promote or encourage violent acts? As the special effects have improved, violence seen on tv or in movies seems much more realistic.

Does the fact that there isn't a specific "prime time" when more violent shows are shown have an effect on violent acts in America? There was a time when tv shows and movies that were considered appropriate for "adults" were only shown in the later evening hours. Nowadays, anyone can watch any tv show, movie, etc., no matter how violent, at almost any time.

Do entertainment events such as mixed martial arts and boxing encourage people to commit violent acts? As a kid I watched professional wrestling, but many of the wrestlers weren't in the same shape as those of today and the action in and out of the ring is certainly different. All of the action seems so much more realistic. Does that encourage violence?

You knew this was coming, but do violent video games lead to real violence? What evidence can you share that supports how you feel about this?

How about famous "role models"? Do threats and/or actions of those in the news lead to more violent actions? There was a time when bullying, threatening, or even physical confrontations were unheard of in a society where courtesy and decency were viewed as the norm. Now, it seems as if disagreements are addressed by confrontation. Is this encouraged, either intentionally or unintentionally, by celebrities?

We often hear about gangs committing violent acts. Why do gangs exist? Is violence always part of gang culture?

What role do parents play, if any, in raising children to choose less confrontational means to address disagreements? Do parents have any responsibility regarding the viewing habits of children?

Does our justice system "encourage" violence, although not intentionally, by not effectively punishing those who commit violent acts?

Sports and the athletes who participate in them have changed. In addition to MMA and boxing that I mentioned above, sports such as football and hockey, among others, seem to include more violence. Athletes are bigger and stronger than when I was growing up, injuries are more prevalent, and violence seems to be expected and tolerated, or even encouraged, more.

Adults, in addition to children, have more devices available to view or listen to more violent actions than existed when I was growing up. Instead of just having a tv, cell phones, tablets, etc. all allow the viewer access to violent media at any time of the day or night. Does this have any effect on the level of violence we see in society?

What role does social media play in encouraging or modeling violence?

25

EDUCATION IN AMERICA

Before any introduction or questions regarding education in America, it's important for you to know that I was a teacher for twenty-five years and a principal for five. I'd like to think that I'm not too biased in my thinking regarding education and schools, but readers may find that to be inaccurate.

Let my bias begin! I think that many of the problems we face in America today can, and should, be addressed with more of an emphasis on schooling and education. As a teacher, I addressed in an ongoing fashion topics such as racism, bullying, kindness, etc. Do these remain as issues Americans may want to address?

Finally, because I view education as key to America's success as a world leader, I've broken down the sections in this chapter by topics. Then again, it may be because there are so many aspects to education that I didn't want to just list questions randomly.

School Subjects

QUESTIONS:

I remember when schools were supposed to focus on the three "r's"- reading, writing, and arithmetic. Should that be the case? Are schools trying to do too much? If so, why is that?

Many citizens feel that there are certain topics that should be added to the school curriculum. I've seen articles mentioning the need for topics such as personal finance, taking care of a residence, doing your taxes, etc. Should these be the responsibility of teachers?

Who determines what is taught at each grade level? Who should determine school curriculum?

If items are added to the curriculum, should something else be dropped? What would that be?

Public Schools, Charter Schools, Private Schools

QUESTIONS:

How should we determine which children attend the different types of schools? Should parents be the sole decision makers?

Should tax payer dollars be used to finance a private school education? How about a charter school education?? What accountability should there be, if any, to ensure those tax payer dollars are used appropriately? Who determines what "appropriate spending" is?

What are the advantages and disadvantages in having your child attend a charter school or a private school?

What are the strengths and weaknesses in public schools? How can those issues be addressed?

Home Schooling (this seems to be a growing trend in education so I've listed it separately)

QUESTIONS:

Like other schooling options, who determines whether a child is home schooled or not?

Should tax payer dollars be given to home schooling parents? Should there be any accountability regarding how the money is spent?

Should home schooled students be allowed to participate in extra curricular activities, such as sports, concerts, etc. that are provided by their local public school district?

What are your thoughts on home-schooling? Should there be guidelines on what is taught? Should parents who home school their children have any requirements as to what they teach? What about standardized testing? How is it determined whether a home schooled child advances to the next grade? Who would decide on those requirements?

Who pays for supplies if you decide to home school your children?

Why do parents decide to home-school their children? What role does religion, school shootings, perceptions of class size, etc. play in those decisions?

Controversial Topics

QUESTIONS:

Who determines what books and other reading materials are available for students? If a parent or group of parents feel that a particular book is not appropriate for children, what steps should they take? Who should they talk to? How should they share their concerns?

If you want a religious education for your child, what choices should you have? Should that take place in a private school? A public school? Should religious instruction only be part of a home schooling curriculum? If you feel that religious instruction should be part of public schooling, what about kids that believe in a different religion? How about kids who don't participate in any formal religion?

If you have a question, concern, or complaint with your child's educational program who do you contact? What if that person doesn't address your question, etc. in a satisfactory manner? When, if ever, is it okay to bring your unhappiness to social media or local media outlets?

Who is responsible when a child is bullied? What steps should be taken if your child experiences bullying?

Do you really know what tenure is for teachers? What are the positives and negatives of tenure? What changes, if any, would you make regarding tenure?

How would you define Critical Race Theory? Do you believe that CRT (Critical Race Theory) is taught in our schools? If so, what specific evidence do you have that supports your beliefs?

As far as I'm aware, public schools have teacher unions. What are the positives and negatives of teacher unions? Does the existence of a teacher union affect children's learning? How?

Who do you trust more when it comes to a child's education, the child's parent or a teacher? What are your reasons for your choice?

What rights should parents have when it comes to their child's learning? Should they determine what materials are used in the classroom? Should they be involved in hiring educators? How about policies regarding student dress or extra curricular activities?

Many schools now provide breakfast and after school programs for students whose parents may need assistance in those areas. Should schools be expected to provide these services? What about simply extending the school day so these areas are part of the "normal" school day?

26

HOLIDAYS

While it's true that holidays don't really change much, how we perceive them and celebrate them does change. Christmas is a Christian holiday and is widely seen as celebrated throughout America, yet I grew up enjoying a day off on Columbus Day and that's not universally recognized anymore. Friends recently shared that certain holidays that aren't as widely celebrated as Christmas now result in days off from school. Then there's Indigenous People's Day, which I'd guess most Americans don't know much about, Dr. Martin Luther King, Jr.'s birthday, which is celebrated in every state now, but wasn't initially, and what some refer to as President's Week, which is when we recognize the birthdays of both President Washington and President Lincoln. Holidays that are identified with a specific religion have become talking points, with some schools opting to recognize them with a day off from school, while others do not.

QUESTIONS:
  Is there actually a "war on Christmas" like I've heard?
  Is it ok to wish someone a Merry Christmas?

Why do some people say Happy Holidays instead of Merry Christmas?

What is Indigenous People's Day?

Why do we not celebrate Columbus Day as a national holiday in every state? Why do some states celebrate some form of a holiday recognizing native people instead of Columbus?

How do we determine what "holidays" should be days off from school or work?

Growing up, I knew about different holidays mostly because of the school calendar. Obviously, I knew about the big ones, like Christmas and Easter, but I didn't know much about some of the others, such as Veterans Day. Still, it seems to me that the school calendar is still the go to resource for holiday information simply because that's often the place where children learn about each specific holiday. However, one question that has become more of an issue in recent years is whether certain holidays mean one or more days off from school.

Consider each of the following holidays loosely listed in the order as they appear on a typical school calendar. Which, if any, should be recognized as worthy of one or more days off from school? ***I apologize if there is a holiday I missed that you may celebrate or recognize in some way.**

Labor Day
Rosh Hashanah
Yom Kippur
Columbus Day
Indigenous Peoples Day
Halloween
Election Day
Veteran's Day
Thanksgiving
Christmas
Kwanzaa
Hanukkah

New Years Day
Chinese New Year
Dr. Martin Luther King, Jr.'s birthday
Valentine's Day
Abraham Lincoln's birthday
George Washington's birthday
St. Patrick's Day
Easter
Passover
Memorial Day
Flag Day
June Nineteenth
Independence Day

27

CELEBRITIES- REAL AND "WANNABES"

I don't think that I'm the only one who feels this way, but I've often imagined myself as a famous celebrity. When I was growing up, I dreamed of becoming a professional athlete. I played tennis quite a bit, but certainly wasn't going to go pro, I played baseball and football, and I think I was pretty good at the sports we played in gym class and in the neighborhood, but that was about it. I don't sing very well and never in public. I have a poor memory for remembering lines and can't act, so the closest I ever came to performing was when I was a "flyer" when I was a school principal and our district was putting on Peter Pan. My job was to pull a cable that enabled one of the characters to "fly" across the stage. I won't share how that worked out, but suffice to say, I didn't go into a career in the performing arts. All of that leads me to this point. I believe that we are absolutely enamored with celebrities in America, regardless of whether it be athletes, singers, actors, etc.

QUESTIONS:
Are we too interested in the lives of "famous people"? What are some of the reasons why this may be the case?

What sources of information do you use in order to find out more about celebrities? Like me, do you simply Google about those you find interesting? Is social media a source for you? How about those magazines that are in the checkout lines in stores?

Are you in any kind of "fan club" or some other group that focuses on a specific celebrity?

How do you react to news that a favorite celebrity of yours is in legal or criminal trouble? Does that affect how you view that individual?

Which celebrities do you admire the most? Why is that?

Which celebrities do you have negative views of? Why is that?

I sometimes read about the income or salaries of certain celebrities or about their somewhat extravagant lifestyles. Do you envy them in any way? For example, what is your reaction when a famous individual buys a private island or a second, third, or fourth home costing millions of dollars?

If you were to become famous, what would it be for? Acting ability? Athletic skills?

Do you think celebrities, as a whole, are paid fairly for what they do for a living?

Are celebrities treated the same way as the "average citizen"? Why or why not?

Are you swayed in any way when a celebrity endorses a product, a politician, etc.? Does it depend on who the celebrity is?

Do you consider those who appear in a realty tv series to be celebrities?

28

PARENTING

With three children now in their thirties, I know enough about being a parent to know none of us are perfect. My wife and I just tried to do our best when it came to our kids in school, their friendships, manners, etc. One advantage we had was that our kids weren't exposed to factors such as cell phones, social media, and gun violence the way many children are today. What's especially scary is that it was still tough being a good parent.

No judging here, but think about how you are as a parent, grandparent, or anyone that is in daily contact with children. Take a good, hard look at your interactions with kids and if you think you're doing a good job.

QUESTIONS:

Do you use appropriate language around kids? Obviously, I'm referring to swearing, but also being verbally respectful and kind to them and others with the way you speak.

How successful are you in following the "golden rule"? In other words, do you treat your children in a kind and respectful way, the way you want to be treated?

Do you have rules for your kids regarding cell phone use, social media that they may be participating in, television, videos, video games, etc. Do you actually follow through with these rules?

Do you follow similar rules yourself?

Are you consistent with any disciplinary actions you may take when your rules or directions aren't followed?

How involved are you in your children's education? Do you attend school events, such as conferences with teachers? Do you help with or check homework? Do you generally show interest in your child's school experiences?

Do you know who your child's friends are? Have you met them and their parents?

Are parents responsible for their kids actions? It may seem like I'm referring to extreme acts by your child, but what about something as simple as talking back to a teacher or other adult?

29

DEAR FORMER STUDENTS

I was a teacher for most of my career, except five years as an elementary school principal. If I could gather all of my former students in a room- make that a stadium- I would address them with the following message:

Dear Kids,

When I began teaching back in the 1980's, I thought being a good role model for all of you was important. After all, as your teacher, I couldn't very well expect you to be nice to your classmates if I wasn't nice, as well. I also tried to model being respectful, honest, and fair. I think you get the idea.

Over the years, whether I was one of your elementary teachers, or the guy who helped you with subjects you found difficult in any grade, I tried to continue to be the teacher who guided you, at least for the year(s) I was your teacher. Being compassionate and humble, and also appreciative of others was important, I thought, and I tried to be the adult who behaved that way. It wasn't always easy and I was far from perfect, but I tried, because those qualities would help you to be successful as you grew up, both as a student and as a person.

I probably shared with you in our classroom how I always liked kids more than adults. That's never really changed and I think it's because kids don't carry as much baggage. Adults have gone through more "stuff", I find, and are more likely to follow the "do as I say and not as I do" philosophy.

I'd like to think, now that you're quite a bit older, that you've held on to some of those values that I tried to model and encourage. I hope you're a kind person, that you try to treat others as you want to be treated- at least most of the time. In this day and age, it seems that an awful lot of people think it's ok to treat others badly, that lying and cheating are just what everyone does, and that following any version of the Golden Rule doesn't really apply to "real life". I hope that's not you. I really do.

Mr. Sack

ABOUT THE AUTHOR

Jim Sack worked with kids for over thirty years, mostly as a teacher, but with a dash of school principal thrown in. His books, sprinkled with humor, are meant to help the reader understand different perspectives and the experiences of others.

Personally, Jim, his wife, Eileen, and their cat, Kenzie, who is always getting into trouble, live in upstate New York not far from their adult children.

www.jimsack.com

facebook.com/jimsacktheauthor
instagram.com/jimsacktheauthor
linkedin.com/in/jim-sack-28171160